Flights of Fancy?

To / waldo

with very best wishes

from Steve

Flights of Fancy?

Steven Foyster
Poems 1991-2023

PAUL DICKSON BOOKS

Flights of Fancy?
Steven Foyster, Poems 1991-2023

Published by Paul Dickson Books September 2023

Paul Dickson Books, 156 Southwell Road, Norwich NR1 3RP
t. 01603 666011
e. paul@pauldicksonbooks.co.uk
www.pauldicksonbooks.co.uk

ISBN: 978-1-7397154-4-1

A CIP catalogue record for this booklet is available from the British Library.

Designed by Brendan Rallison
Illustrations by Roger Foyster
Printed in Norwich by GoWise Print

PUBLISHER'S PREFACE

I am very pleased to present Steven Foyster's collection of poems, written between 1991 and 2023. Steven writes in a very accessible and enjoyable way. The themes are varied, as he responds to the world around him.

Writing poetry has undoubtedly helped him in the long recovery since he jumped off St Andrew's Car Park in Norwich in 1986, aiming to kill himself. Steven's humour and resilience shines through his poetry, as it does in his book *Cry to be Heard!, My Road to Recovery*, which I published in September 2021.

Paul Dickson
Norwich
July 2023

CONTENTS

Author's Introduction

I first started jotting down bits of poetry in my teens. Looking back on some recently they didn't read particularly well.

I started composing the earliest in this collection in the 1990s, often during the rail journeys whilst commuting from Norwich to Ipswich.

Although these only took about 45 minutes each way they seemed to give my mind a blank piece of paper to work on, jotting down ideas and frameworks to be completed usually within a day or so. Of course the regularity of delayed trains, often up to an hour gave me more time for thought!

I didn't write much more for over twenty years. However, the concept of publication discussed during the past year or so prompted me to write again . Some of those, such as ' Trees Be Without You' and ' Dysfunctional Unity', sadly reflect the state of the world at the moment.

I do find writing poetry cathartic, especially when going through a bad periods of physical pain which can often become entangled with mental distress.

I am exceptionally grateful to my brother, Roger, for stunning illustrations and to Paul Dickson for publishing these poems, many of which have been languishing in folders for thirty years

Steven Foyster
Norwich
July 2023

1

FLIGHTS OF FANCY

When I am tired
In flights of fancy
Oft I dream
That I should die
to stalk the streets
to beat the bounds
to reign supreme!

Disguised by death
I'll fool my friends
Not what I seem
I could offend
Now skulking sweetly
Perfect pounce
I'll draw some blood
and savour screams!

Camouflaged
The eyes do glint with emerald green
that watch for hours
with baited breath
to lure the prey
in confidence
to not be seen

The fur will fly
and gore be spilt
I'll claw the life
from trembling hearts
and bring my bounty
to your door
the cat who spilt the cream!

22 July 1993

I'm not sure where this came from. Retyping it reminds me a little of the film 'Cat People', but hardly as dark.

LOVE

Love is patient for the good
Impatient to rid evil

Love accepts others as they are

Love cares
Love hopes
Love hurts

Love is taking the risk
taking the blame
taking defeat in good humour

Love is selfless, not self-inflicting
honest without being cruel
daring without being blind

Love is an anger
Love is a need
Love is a prayer
Love is a deed

Love is openness and vulnerability
Love is not nailing a man to a cross, but the forgiveness that flows from it

Love is life
Love is good
Love is God

1991 (with amendments 2021)

HOPE

From the womb of our creator
We are dragged, reluctant
Screaming

In the cradle of mankind
Peace be with you
Dreaming

To the warmth of the breast
Milk of human kindness
Succour
With the first hopes of our future
There is a word
Mumma

And now we're running home from school
To please our elders is the rule
Top marks in maths again today
My brand new coat has gone astray
Envy

Trying hard to please my peers
With deeds that must not reach the ears
Of parents, teachers and the rest
This smoking's not good for my chest
Scheming

I met this boy, he's rather rough
He owns a car, and god he's tough
The way he looks me in the eyes
I wish he'd take me for his prize

We're going steady, what a date!
My dad just loathes him, which is great
He drives to fast and holds me tight
No-one can tell me this ain't right

A cottage by the sea
Just him and me
Dreaming

It wasn't how it should have been
The earth stayed still for him and me
He hadn't even come to tea
If dad finds out he'll murder me!

I'm ten days late, it can't get worse
I'm praying for the bloody curse!
And he won't see me any more
It seems he's found another 'score'

Caught inside a tightening web
It's bursting my head
Screaming!!

I told mum and she told dad
He went crazy, she was sad
They will help me all they can
But I'm bereft of any man

Joanna Mary
7lb 6 oz
Screaming

I will watch you day and night
Soothe your tears and hold you tight
I will love you all my days
I won't let you go astray

Dreaming …

February 1992

FAITH

I know you're there
Though I can't see you
Feel your presence
Sense your sile
Won't you tell us
Why you left us
So alone
For all this while

Why are we here?
Why the doubt?
What's this living all about?
Was it worth it?
Will you tell us?
All the anguish, bloodied tears
Have we just been treading water
For the last two thousand years?

I know you're there
Yet I can't see you
Feel your presence
Sense your smile
Won't you give us
Just an inkling
That you'll be back
In a while?

All this suffering
Rampant evil
No must trust and daily horror
We need you here
Or we won't make it
Sodom's back like no Gomorrah!
Love is now a well-worn cliché
Retail-packed and ribbon wrapped
If we can't get back to basics
Something somewhere is going to snap

I know you're there
When I can't see you
Feel your presence
Sense your smile
I know you'll be back
When we're ready
Once we use faith as a child

February 1992

CHASM

The gulf is so wide
yet the way so narrow
A smile
a hug
simple love
Might defeat
the hurt
the need

'They' of course are fanatics!
like 'our' crusaders, give or take a millennium
but such atrocities!
No worse than ours

Quick to chide, slow to bless,
small wonder the world is a bloodied mess

The Moslem child coughing
thirsting, dying
cries to the same God

Suffer the little children,
don't make them suffer

There is no hope in religion
there is no hope in greed
the greatest satanic vice

October 1991
Reflections on the Gulf War

THAT'S LIFE

Harlow Town
Sunday April 12th
Marathon Day

A miniature person
Called Ashley
bedecked in Aztec duffle
red baseball cap
and mittens
Descends the mountain of British Rail stairs
engulfed by the enormity of it all
The digital station clock
Packages
Every
Second
Of being

Stanstead express eats the air
' Tain! Tain!' he yells
Gone in a flash
Like life
But the singing of the rails
Holds fast the vision
Like the spirit
of a dead friend
sharing a memory

April 1992

Dedicated to a dear friend Ray Lowe who took me to Anfield when I was wheelchair bound
as a 30th birthday present. Even in death we may never walk alone.

ARE WE NOT WORTHY?

In Birmingham
I met a ragged man
Who'd walked many ragged miles
Who wished he had a sixpence
Let alone a sense of style
Tattered trousers
tattered mind
tattered life
Foraging in the litter bin of existence
for other people's burger dregs
last mouthful from discarded cans
Muttering
muttering
not mattering
Just worthy to gather up the crumbs
from under other's tables

And as I pressed a pound coin
into his filthy hand
His thank-you smile
Lit up his universe
and mine
A smile of resurrection
From a crucified Christ
It made me sad
it made me cry
it gave me hope

May 1992

I had just spent an hour at an interview for a position within a Christian youth charity.
All I had been asked again and again, was if and how I'd been 'saved'. I couldn't give an
answer. Surely we all have a daily choice. Thankfully I wasn't offered the job! Yet being
released into the sunshine still left me shattered and somewhat angry I suppose.
How could the message of the gospels be distorted into theological hoop-jumping?
Then I saw the man ...

M-I-A-O-W!

Yowls from the rooftops
Two in the morn
Bleary-eyed sleepers
Curse 'Bugger off home!'
Sentries at sunrise
Displaying dead gifts
Sparrows at breakfast
Cause family rifts
Mewing for munchies
Clawing at knees
Feline impatience
Never say please!
Wind up the buskins
Stirred by the gale
Instant amusement
Chasing your tail
First to the fireplace
Favourite spot
How can you bear it
so furnacy hot?
Flickering eyelids
comfiest lap
Day has been tiring
time for a nap
You know you're the cat's whiskers, don't you?

Spring 1992

Have warmed to cats in recent years having grown up with an extraordinarily energetic retriever cross. I do remember seeing a cat sprawled out in maternal grandfather's stifling hot greenhouse in temperatures close to 100 fahrenheit and wondering why he didn't self-combust!

LET US RETURN

Do you remember when it snowed so hard
That you could hear the silence?
When it covered your lace-holes
Trees became shapes without form
Icicles drooped from the gutters
We all cleared the paths
Neighbours shopped
Strangers chatted
The world was at one
When evening fell
Shovelling aches soothed
Hot baths, hot cocoa, hot toddies
The magic of it all
Reflected in the embered grate
Let us return, let us return
Before it is all too late

Do you remember when it was so hot
You could hear the grasshoppers chipping?
You made a tent over the washing line
With an old double sheet and some twine
You feasted inside on biscuits and lemonade
The sun shone every day
Delivery men whistled
Grandma got sunburnt
And the world shone
In bed that night
You counted and recounted in your head
Pennies saved for the trip
The excitement of it all
Trains, sand, kites that soared
Donkey rides, shrimp pools, waves that roared
Let us go back, let us go back
Tell me it's not too late

Do you remember reading once
How God came down to earth as man?
Hope covered the world
History became now, vision became truth

Enemies hugged in the light
Fishermen were kings
The poor were blessed
He washed our feet
And all was one
When darkness fell
And the knives were out
Torn in two on a bleeding cross
All seemed lost
Yet the flame wouldn't die
In the hearts of his friends
Who cared and shared
Dared to believe in the shadow of death
Let us return, let us return
He tells us it's never too late

July 1992

PRINCE OF TIDES

The seaside is where I first found God,
Walking the spume drenched promenade
Waves lashing thirty feet of anger
against man-made barricades
" Why won't you let me in?
Why won't you let me into your lives?
I'm normally so peaceful and calm"

A giant to be wrestled with
Never tamed
" Why won't you let me in?
I let you play with me
Listen to my song
Still you shut me out"

Giver of unfathomable riches
Simply requesting respect
" Why won't you let me in?
I let you dive to my very soul
Of myriad colours
Still you shut me out
with your pathetic barriers
Do you not realise that I could tear them all to shreds
The flow is too one way!
Unless you become like fishermen
You will never understand
It is time to let down your nets".

August 1992

I love the silence found in empty churches and the beauty of many cathedrals. However
I first discovered an inkling of God at a beach on the Norfolk coast. Nature, man and the
holy spirit as one would indeed be a blessed trinity.

TREES BE WITH YOU!

Dripping willows weep
Wrinkled oaks keep
watch o'er England's history
Graveyard peaceful yews
Larches limp with morning dew
Sylvan magic mystery

Snow-white paper birches
Single blackthorn lurches
from raw prevailing wind
Rubied rowans, jewels glowing,
Redwing's favourite find

Swaying poplar lines
Scented skyward pines
Frosted, feathered, festive firs,
Sun-kissed beeches
Homes to creatures
Nooks where nature stirs

Youngsters scrape lithe legs
Scrambling for discarded eggs
Straddling boughs; grazing knees,
Palettes catch the scene
A thousand shades of verdant green
The wonder found in trees

Boxing Day 1992

I can't remember why I happened to write this on Boxing Day. My parents both loved trees, especially my father who ensured that a wide range which still thrive were planted on the field of a high school he designed in the 1970s. I presented my parents with a framed copy of this poem as a joint birthday present one September, with beautiful calligraphy and illustrations by my brother Roger.

C-H-A-I-N-E-D

ANGERENDINGROWNMENEUTERED
NERVESTRIPPEDOWN TO NAKED FEAR
LIFETIMESTIFLED MIXED EMOTIONS
CLENCH A FIST TO SHED A TEAR
HOLDOWNASTYEARNING SOBBING
BREAK A PROMISE- SMASH A FACE
TOUGHEARTRICKING LYING ROBBING
CALLOUSED HANDS THEIRIGHTFUL PLACE
DRUNKENIGHTSO MAD IT'S FRIGHTENING
CHILDRENEVEROCKED TO SLEEP
CURSES THREATS DEMANDS AND BEATINGS
ALL BECAUSE YOU CANNOT WEEP

13 February 1993

I wrote this whilst working for Suffolk Social Services. The social workers and managers discovered some terrible incidents of physical and emotional abuse, mainly carried out by men. This poem doesn't excuse any such actions but perhaps touches on an underlying cause in some cases, often sadly carried down from one generation to another.

FAITH 'n' CHIPS

So much choice
Multi-voice
Karmas, creeds and isms
Right and left
A soul bereft
Splinter groups and schisms
Allah, Yahweh, Buddha, Christ
That's good value for the price!
Cut me off a great big slice
To fill that holy hole

Read the label
Yes that's me!
It's advertised on prime TV
This is the way
So bright and gay
Precious, pretty, oh so glossy
Packaging conceals the vice
It's so hygienic, looks so nice
But doesn't make me whole

So shop around
You may confound
The market leader's guiles
Spend 'n' save
Each brand you crave
Taste them for a while
Eternal opening's here to stay
The aisles should lead us all one-way
To bread of life that shouts Oy Vey!
Faith's a mulit-flavoured roll

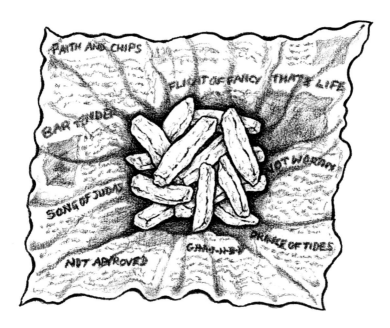

28 April 1993 (with amendments February 2023)

I've found that some Christians are really hung up on other faiths. I've only explored Christianity. Yet I could find solace in the Buddhist way (although not a 'faith') through meditation, emphasising the preciousness of all life. I admire the Moslem disciplines of prayer and fasting. I've found that over the years certain 'brands' of Christianity advertise, often forcefully that their particular way of belief and interpretation of biblical text is the only way to salvation. Exploitation and terrible abuse has run rife for many centuries in the name of Christianity. More recently distorting certain lines of the Koran has led to the most extreme violence. I hope that all faiths lead one way; to acceptance, humility, kindness and forgiveness.

RAIN

I think I hear the rain
Yes, here it is
Smidgens of patter
Breaking to
gobbing splatter,
Strafing the pane

Quite strange
As we have waited so long
For the storm
to break
That my listening ached
For the change

Thunder beckons
Drapes drawn wide
Torrents lash outside
Slide the sash
Gulp the wind
It billows out
My weathered doubt

Do I cry in vain
to a cruel God who thrived on flood?
On nights like these
It does me good
To drown in heaven's rain

28 May 1993

It hadn't rained for weeks. Suddenly the drought broke in no uncertain terms. It got me thinking about the Biblical flood which I have never been able to reconcile to the love of a non-judgmental Jesus Christ so often exemplified within the gospels.

SO WHERE IS THIS CHRIST?

So where is this Christ?
Show me
Now!
In sad-faced sleepers
Filling pews
Spilling out a pattered creed
Of how it's oh so nice to bleed
I doubt it
Somehow

So where is this Christ?
Show me
Please
In gleaming plate so sparkling clean?
An altered state, a man-made scene
Is He really in there?

So where is this Christ?
Show me
Where
In a cloying holy wafer
That will keep our souls much safer?
Maybe
With prayer

So where is this Christ?
Lead me
There
With loving mothers caught in war
Who wail for children that they bore,
By grieving fathers sharing sadness
Praying they can end the madness
In stick-like people, barely standing
Who seem so very understanding
Believing God will find the means
To satisfy their craving dreams
In patient saints who nurse the dying
When most of us just feel like crying
Tending sores and washing feet
Making last days cool and sweet
In friendly gestures, hugs and smiles
Gurgling chuckles from a child
In righteous anger, loss of hope
In our ability to cope
He is always
There

17 June 1993

Looking back on this I feel I might have been rather harsh to the established church as so
many good people emanate love from within it and do amazing unsung work. However
I think there is a real danger of making any church service like bringing out the Sunday
best whilst Jesus is cleaning out the sewers.

AT THE SEASIDE

Jehovah has opened the skylight
The window is full of the blue
Sunshine absorbing my senses
Creation is brand spanking new
Binoculars scanning the briny horizon
Past freighters now Humberside bound
Divers still searching for maritime secrets
I pray that they'll never be found.

Children and parents are toiling in tandem
A boat carved from tentative sand
Tiny tots clutching their castle-shaped buckets
Pensioners stroll hand-in-hand
Lovers are posing by seaweed strewn groynes
Brushing hot sand from her slacks
Rippling torsos and sun-blistered shoulders
Ladies in flowery hats

Ice-creams are savoured in multiple flavours
Babies hang breastward for dozing
A jet rapes the silence
and breaks the horizon
The picture is no longer frozen.

24 August 1993

Since childhood I have never tired of the wonder of the North Norfolk coastline. This
was written the evening after a visit to West Runton beach, nestling between Cromer and
Sheringham. The scene looked simply perfect, held in space and time. Even lustful lovers
blended almost innocently into an Edenesque way. Then a screeching jet. One moment
of aggression; paradise lost.

NOT APPROVED?

I touched the old school bell
dated 1884
wondered if it held
the years of young resentment
to it's ringing rule

I peered through the knot-holed fence
now obsolete
imagined those years hence
chlorine reek and shivered youths
in an ageing pool

I wandered cross the 'playing' field
still used
believing that the grass could feel
the hatred trod on rigid runs
sodden cruel

on turning back to present views
I saw a broken belt in gutter strewn
symbol of the battered lives
that were once approved

March 1996

I wrote this after a visit to a modern training centre built on the site of an approved
school. 'The Loneliness of the Long Distance Runner' by Alan Sillitoe which I was most
impressed by when I read in my teens, came to mind.

THE OTHER GRASS?

We could believe the slate's wiped clean
on a day as clear as this
If it wasn't for horizons
we would see forever

Our vision would be just as keen
as the kestrel's on the wire
If it wasn't for our human fear
we would take our chance

Our future's strewn before our gaze
the endless fields; the open sky
If it wasn't for our human doubt
we wouldn't wonder whether

The patchwork quilt we call our lives
is set entrenched in furrowed lines
If it wasn't for our human greed
we'd give the global view a chance

We're given oh so much and more
It takes the breath; it fills the soul
If it wasn't for our human flaws
We'd know we have what makes us whole

13 April 1996

Some of this poem started evolving when on a train travelling through rural south
Norfolk, spotting a kestrel on a telegraph wire. I glimpsed it drop so accurately for it's
prey, wondering at it's speed of vision and all too often, humanity's lack of it.

FROM TOP TO TAIL

Life's tapestry is shredded
No cutting of cloth can account for this
on a ragged windswept day
the sun at it's zenith

Washing on the line
whips against my face with unremitting repetition
Torn from pegs
Snagged in trees
Whence the seamless garment
of day-today routine?

Curtain torn from top to tail
Yet as the clothes,
many tattered,
are retrieved
or fall to earth
Can I perceive a pattern
as I fold them from harm's way?

5 September 2002

I received a telephone call about my first wife's suicide whilst running a conference bookstall. Sue had suffered from suicidal tendencies since we first met. We had divorced fifteen years before her death, with hardly any contact. Yet I found the force of the news brutal. I attended her funeral in late August, having arranged a church youth trip to the Theatre Royal Norwich to see ' Joseph' the very next week. I was hardly in the mood. Yet by the finale of a remarkable performance I felt some sort of short-term healing. Maybe any dream would do.

BAR TENDER?

The man at the bar
is trying to ply her a drink
Answers, reassures
He has procured this before
Shares with me the benefits
of Stella Artois
'A man after his own heart'
Perhaps he was a star in his time
before shooting to the ground

The man at the bar
yearns to befriend me,
soul clinging to my edges
I am so tired
of human need
A search for solitude
shuffles me away
shadowed by guilt
yet not a drop spilt

The man at the bar
has befriended another
to smother the search for himself

1 June 2002

I desperately needed a quiet drink. The intrusion of this needy man was simply too
much. In my shame I made myself scarce, sidling to the other side of the pub. I wondered
afterwards if Christ ever feel this way as exemplified in a scene from Jesus Christ
Superstar. I did hope so for my sake.

PRINTEMPS!

Aching adolescent ardour
Birch and beech buds burst from branch
Creaking cruisers cradle quayside
Rain drenched daffies dare to dance
Eager infants Easter egg-hunt
Fillies frolic: feel the force
Giggling girls grope gangling partners
Hay-filled havens; happy horse!
Icy blasts ignore the seasons
Jack Frost jangles aches and pains
Kids cavort with crazy cartwheels
Leaf shade douses dappled lanes
Magic miracle of rebirth
Nature's nestled all this time
Opens up it's age-old secret
Printemps' passion in it's prime!
Queen bees quell the winter doldrums
Runners race round London's lanes
Sweethearts share seductive secrets
Tripping toddlers taste their treats
Umbrellas urgently unfurled
Viva vernal equinox!
Willows weep
Exit winter
Yuletide yearnings
Gone to zzz

I think this was written in 2002, but I have no specific date. I love playing word games including within my brain. My father has always been a great crossword enthusiast. During my time as a bookseller I never ceased to be amazed that so much can be written over so many centuries with the aid of 26 letters and a little bit of nuance!

JUST LISTEN

Listen to the heartbeat of my soul
Listen to the damage that breaks the whole

Listen to the fears that dread my night
Dwell within my darkness, shadowing the light

Life's tapestry unwoven throughout the years
Stitch up my folly and dry up my tears

Raging heat that needs cool balm
Hold my hand, ease off self-harm

Listen to my pleas

Listen to me please

Just listen

7 April 2021

HEAL

Smiles, hugs, touch
Mean so much

Positive honesty
Sheer generosity

Time, and more time, to spare
Holding and healing
A shared feeling

Trust
Just
walking alongside
Providing steps along a road

Gradually leading from darkness to light …

4 April 2022

TIME

Mercury slides, brambles catch
fast bends, slow lanes, planning, shambles
motionless joy
fears that cloy
paradise lost
from innocent gloss
drinking night sessions
floating impressions
of reality
found within the very late
smouldering grate
of expectations
ashes to ashes
dust to dust
imperative dreaming
from maybe to must
photographs, memories
semi-transparent
snapshots of youth
allusion and truth
second hand ticks
minuted changes
hours to share
till time to go .....

12 May 2022

BEAUTY IN CONTEXT

Glowering clouds singly pierced
by strips of heaven's light
above a football stadium
incongruous sight?

Yet what life those oft-filled stands
have witnessed
through generational fans
since 1902

Small ever-regular groups form
communities of care and hope
season in, season out
when children were hoisted shoulder high
to beam in wonder from the front

The oldest football anthem in the world
ringing round so loud
could times be heard miles away

Joy and frustration
Heroes and villains
Heavy old turnstiles
That clicked for a shilling

The 3.00 pm ritual
Long gone since
to cater for corporate greed
yet glimpses of a beautiful game
still shine and mirror life

Maybe not so out of context

6-7th November 2022
Rail/bus journey to Nottingham

DYSFUNCTIONAL UNITY

All the Blatter blather and the Platinitudes
cannot drown out the rancour toward a stitched-up,
riched-up,
rotten state of Qatar
Stale scent of tainted Musk
as twitterings turn to racist rants
Morgan hardly a Freeman
with baseless words
of togetherness division
tainted with hypocritical lucre
Sheik a dice, as heads roll from the the first whistle
A bloody killing spree in injury time
Protesters shot down across the water
players refusing to sing the song
Rainbows clouded by rising storm
To stand so 'straight' and be the 'norm'
The beautiful game never seemed so far
as the world watches on aghast
A football family
of dysfunctional unity

21 November 2022
Second day of World Cup Finals

RUNNING AWAY?

When we seek to travel elsewhere
Are we fleeing from ourselves?
The train of thoughts still running
Not derailed, debunked or shelved,
Shipped away to foreign shores
The thoughts still lap our souls,
Dredged up from distant memories
The same as e'er before
Flotsam, jetsam, effluent flow
Held behind a wall of shame,
Will breach the bank of steadfastness,
Once fear has claimed a name
The points might change, the tide might turn,
Yet travellers carry on,
To bear the baggage, grip the rail,
With no space left to mourn.

3 December 2022

TREES BE WITHOUT YOU

Ripped from your ground
with sickening sounds
of earth grinding
root ripping
chain sawing
leaf shredding death
Silent screams
from bark stripped clean
swaying poplars
hacked 'to size'
Birched and beaten
broken bracken
wildlife flees
their homes in trees
A solitary oak is spared
standing still yet not so proud
with all his neighbours torn away
a sad relentless 'progress' day

10 December 2022

THE TRUE PAIN

Will rip your soul asunder
Tie it back into a Gordian knot
so tight it drags you under
Stultify your dreams
which still pull at the seams
Tear apart your inner self
Nail it to a dusty shelf
Hurt beyond the joints that sear
releasing all the inner fear
The guilt, the sadness,
The loss, the madness
If you've got enough rope
Will it stretch to hope?
To put the darkness to flight
And get you through the night.

13 January 2023

SONG OF JUDAS

No more bright blue brave tomorrows
Past was dead and nothing followed
Now was not enough
Sliding down the slope of hope
Didn't have the grace to cope
Things got far too rough
It wasn't me
it wasn't you
Who crucified our Lord in two
but worthy men
and women too
who didn't have the stuff

God made them leaders
Now their saints
Pentecost held no restraint
to cast out demons
heal the faint
with power from up above
My prayer, my dream
that sometime soon
You'll all come clean
admit that I
was trapped midstream
the tide was far too tough

Men need scapegoats
for their martyrs
Purple hearts
with stars and garters
sing their blessed Alma Mater
whence the peaceful dove?
Cast the dice
and tear the clothes
We could save those
and those ... not those!
Sweet napalm smells
just like a rose
when push comes down to shove
You burn your blame
and bury your guilt
remember precious
blood's been spilt
Let's make sure that
Heaven is built
on rocks hewn out of love

I've always reckoned that Judas got a rough deal. He made a fatal error in betraying Jesus and paid for it by his suicide. If Jesus hadn't been betrayed, would he have been crucified and subsequently resurrected? Maybe. This is an eternal song from Judas trying to persuade the human race not to be too judgmental. He takes a real snipe at the other disciples who ran away and hid, only to become heroes. In his bitterness he doesn't of course recognise the martyrdom of these apostles. Then we leap almost 2,000 years to American foreign policy in the Vietnam War. It often seems that America's decision to intervene and bomb the people of other countries to smithereens is 'right'. God bless America?

HEROES AND VISIONS

John the Baptist
Jesus Christ
Peace on earth
A bowl of rice
Norwich City
Grace and pity
Careful how you go
April showers
Rainbow days
Food and warmth for waifs and strays
Pass the parcel
Pass the parcel
Never let it go!

Love is God
And God is love
Taize chants
A pair of gloves
Honesty with
no more lies
Adios without goodbyes
Inner power
Sweet dreams
Tell a joke and
keep it clean
Fresh baked bread
Fluffy teddies
Lying in the sun

Children's laughter
Cheeky grins
Forgiveness and the end of sin
Keep it going
Keep a troshin'
Never let it stop!
Let it be
With John & Yoko
Late-night films
With cups of cocoa
Warm toes

Jesus rose
He will come again

Communal wine
Baked beans
Peter, Paul and all the 'team'
Sikhs and Hindus
MK Gandhi
Bill & Ben
And Andy Pandy
Chez nous
Chez toi
Carousels
Electric cars
Inner space
Multi-race
Don't keep it in the family

End of famine
Women priests
No more borders
West and east
Holy gospels
'Chuck & Di'
Chocolate ice-cream
Apple pie
No more bombs
No offence
Flower garlands
Frankincense
Start with a mustard seed
End of hate and end of greed

Jimmy Stewart
William Blake
Sex-control and no more rape
National Health
Share the wealth
Take life as it comes
No more dogma
Intercede
Give it to the one in need

Jesus help me
Don't desert me!
Take me as I am

Ramadan
Noah's ark
Two by two
Public parks
Olympic games
With proper aims
Stronger, faster, higher!
Father, Son & Holy Ghost
Try our best
To make the most
Robert Geldoff
Saint Theresa
Chariots of Fire

Shining hair
And summer dresses
Twinkling eyes
And soft caresses
Mary Poppins
Local shopping
Cameras sometimes lie
Patrick Moore
And Haley's comet
Fred Astaire
With Easter bonnets
Lenny Henry
William Foyster
Truth in someone's eyes

Natural tans
Friends and lovers
Cherry blossom
Duvet covers
Breaking walls
But mending fences
Shaking hands
without pretences
Midnight mass

Easter Sunday
Keep it going when it's Monday
Love and nature all around us
Holy spirit please surround us

Peter Sellars
John Cleese
Saying thank you
Saying please
Revelation
Fiery passion
Cool-ed by the breeze
Adam, Eve
without the blushes
Baby found amongst the rushes
Give and take
Love that aches
Plant a million trees!

Making love
Touching hands
Jokes and giggles
Son of Man
Silent prayer
Single glazing
Lots of singing!
Lots of praising!
Willy Brandt
Gorbachev
Smiling faces
Beat the odds
Change the world
When we're able
Helpless babe born in a stable

Communication
Less frustration
Equal rights
Emancipation
No pollution
Green solutions
Paradise ahead
Please don't worry

Have a care
Light a candle
Someone's there
Integration
Firm foundations
Roof above our heads

Graham Kendrick
Joyful psalms
Winding rivers
Lindisfarne
R2D2
Carpe diem!
Calming of the storm
Slow to chide
Yet swift to bless
Let's clear up this bloodied mess
Joseph's dreams
Sparkling streams
The door, the bread, the vine

MLK
Lady Jane
Let His suffering
Ease the pain
Virgin birth
Touch the earth
The faith of Abraham
Make me happy
Make me weep
Gentle massage
Peaceful sleep
Anfield's sadness
No more madness
Never walk alone!

Simple sermons
Gospel preachers
Love your neighbour
Cream and peaches
Eric Morecambe
Little Ern

Let a sense of humour reach us
Total freedom !
No more guilt
Remember that His blood was spilt
Imperfection
Resurrection
Raise us to our knees

Unlocked churches
Synagogues
Christmas crackers
Yuletide logs
Jimmy Connors
Hope and honour
Soothing cups of tea
Have a voice
Take your pick
Kiss me slowly
Kiss me quick
See a stranger
Call him brother
Whatever happens, love each other!

No date for this one! I really like Billy Joel's songs and this was written in response to listening We Didn't Light the Fire, many times starting when I was recuperating in Mundesley Physiotherapy Rehab Unit in 1986. Although I found the lyrics very incisive eventually they came over as rather negative so wrote this to have a beat to it and read or spoken very quickly. William Foyster is my paternal grandfather who inspired me both when alive and after he passed away in 1971.

Cry to be Heard!

My Road to Recovery

Steven Foyster

"All life is here - and that includes death and eternity."

Brian Thorne

www.pauldicksonbooks.co.uk